SandCastle

Silent Letters

silent l
as in chalk

Carey Molter

Consulting Editor Monica Marx, M.A./Reading Specialist

ABDO
Publishing Company

Published by SandCastle™, an imprint of ABDO Publishing Company, 4940 Viking Drive, Edina, Minnesota 55435.

Printed in the United States.

Credits
Edited by: Pam Price
Curriculum Coordinator: Nancy Tuminelly
Cover and Interior Design and Production: Mighty Media
Photo Credits: BananaStock Ltd., Brand X Pictures, Eyewire Images, Hemera, PhotoDisc, Rubberball Productions

Library of Congress Cataloging-in-Publication Data

Molter, Carey, 1973-
    Silent L as in chalk / Carey Molter.
       p. cm. -- (Silent letters)
    Includes index.
    Summary: Easy-to-read sentences introduce words that contain a silent "L," such as chalk, yolk, and talk.
    ISBN 1-59197-447-X
      1. English language--Consonants--Juvenile literature. [1. English language--Consonants.] I. Title.

PE1159.M657 2003
428.1--dc21

2003048125

SandCastle™ books are created by a professional team of educators, reading specialists, and content developers around five essential components that include phonemic awareness, phonics, vocabulary, text comprehension, and fluency. All books are written, reviewed, and leveled for guided reading, early intervention reading, and Accelerated Reader® programs and designed for use in shared, guided, and independent reading and writing activities to support a balanced approach to literacy instruction.

Let Us Know

After reading the book, SandCastle would like you to tell us your stories about reading. What is your favorite page? Was there something hard that you needed help with? Share the ups and downs of learning to read. We want to hear from you! To get posted on the ABDO Publishing Company Web site, send us e-mail at:

sandcastle@abdopub.com

SandCastle Level: Beginning

Silent-l Words

calf

chalk

palm

talk

walk

yolk

3

Jan writes on the sidewalk with chalk.

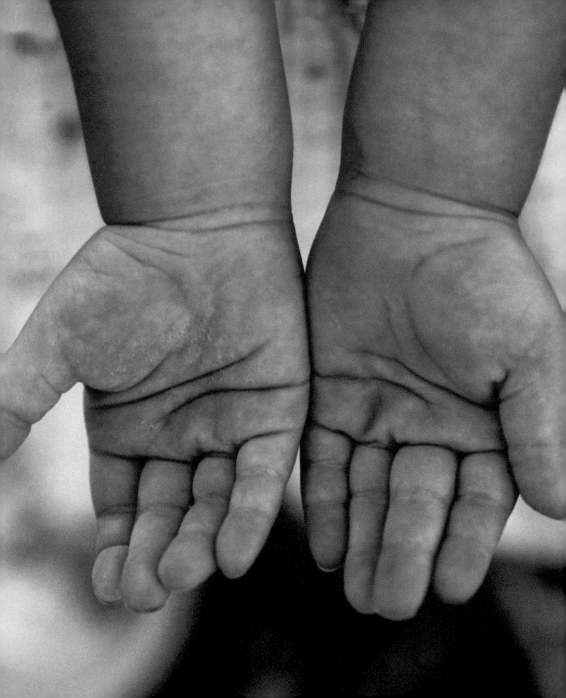

The inside, flat
part of your hand
is called the
palm.

The Carters
walk in the grass.

The **yolk** is the yellow part of the egg.

A calf is
a baby cow.

Trish likes to talk
on the phone.

The Little Calf's Chalk

The little calf took a walk.

She found some chalk
while on her walk.

Bessie

She could write her name.

She should play a game.

But she met her friend Jack

and chose to walk back.

More Silent-l Words

balk

caulk

folk

half

salmon

would

Glossary

calf a baby cow, elephant, or whale

chalk a powdery stick used for writing on sidewalks and blackboards

palm the inside part of your hand between your wrist and your fingers

sidewalk a paved path for walking beside a street

yolk the yellow part of an egg

About SandCastle™

A professional team of educators, reading specialists, and content developers created the SandCastle™ series to support young readers as they develop reading skills and strategies and increase their general knowledge. The SandCastle™ series has four levels that correspond to early literacy development in young children. The levels are provided to help teachers and parents select the appropriate books for young readers.

Emerging Readers
(no flags)

Beginning Readers
(1 flag)

Transitional Readers
(2 flags)

Fluent Readers
(3 flags)

These levels are meant only as a guide. All levels are subject to change.

To see a complete list of SandCastle™ books and other nonfiction titles from ABDO Publishing Company, visit **www.abdopub.com** or contact us at:

4940 Viking Drive, Edina, Minnesota 55435 • 1-800-800-1312 • fax: 1-952-831-1632